The

NEPHILIM DECEPTION

A SCRIPTURAL REFUTATION OF THE
FALSE TEACHING THAT FALLEN ANGELS
MATED WITH HUMAN FEMALES TO
PRODUCE GENETIC GIANTS

The
NEPHILIM DECEPTION

**A SCRIPTURAL REFUTATION OF THE
FALSE TEACHING THAT FALLEN ANGELS
MATED WITH HUMAN FEMALES
TO PRODUCE GENETIC GIANTS**

Cover artwork by mikegi @Pixabay.com

By C.M. Boyer

Former writer and editor for Fortune 100
Companies operating internationally.
Former U.S. Government Operational
Intelligence Analyst.

The NEPHILIM DECEPTION
First Edition 2016

© **2016 C.M. Boyer. All Rights Reserved.** Except as permitted by the Copyright Act of 1976, no part of this publication may be reproduced, stored in a retrieval system or transmitted in any form or by any means without the prior written permission of the publisher.

Boyer, C.M.
The NEPHILIM DECEPTION / by C.M. Boyer
1.United States. 2. Non-fiction.
ISBN-13: 978-1523790791
ISBN-10: 1523790792
Publisher: Create Space Independent Publishing Platform, an Amazon company.

INTRODUCTION

Lately the false doctrine that Nephilim (the alleged "giants" in the Old Testament) are a result of fallen angels/demons mating with human females has permeated latter day Christianity, with the false doctrine being promoted on popular Christian websites.

The internet, wide knowledge of the existence of the Book of Enoch, the Hollywood movie Noah, among other things, has helped to propagate the false teaching of demon-human reproduction.

The false doctrine appeals to people with "itchy ears" as 2 Timothy 4:3 attests:

"For the time will come when they will not endure sound doctrine; but after their own lusts shall they heap to themselves teachers, having itching ears."

Those who will believe anything have turned from the truth as 2 Timothy 4:4 warns

"And they shall turn away their ears from the truth, and shall be turned unto fables."

Christians who mislead people on Nephilim twist the plainest statements in Scripture to fit their fanciful imagination. They appear to be spreading this false doctrine in order to sell books, downloads or other merchandise, and to attract followers who will donate to their coffers.

The false teaching that demons mated with human females to produce the "giants" mentioned in the Old Testament is un-scientific, Biblically unsound, and satanic in nature. Herein this false belief is termed "Nephilim Nonsense."

I believe that upon finishing this book there will be no doubt in the reader's mind that fallen angels cannot and have not mated with human females.

OVERVIEW

Main Fallacies of Nephilim Nonsense promoters:

- Fallen angels are the "sons of God" named in Job;
- fallen angels took on human form in order to mate with human females;
- this demon-human mating created the "giants" or Nephilim mentioned in the Old Testament;
- God sent the Noachian Flood because of this alleged demon-human mating;
- fallen angel DNA exists in the human population today because God is incompetent and didn't destroy everyone but Noah and his family in the Flood.
- Jude and 2 Peter speak of fallen angels "going after strange flesh";
- the book of Enoch is like Scripture and should be taken seriously;

This book presents scientific and Scriptural evidence refuting the above. Main points in each Chapter:

CHAPTER 1
- The biological, physical and creative impossibility of demon-female human reproduction.

CHAPTER 2
- The "sons of God" in Scripture always refer to humans, not fallen angels.

CHAPTER 3
- Old Testament "Giants" are not hybrids, but include all pre-Flood humans.

CHAPTER 4
- "Daughters of men" are from Cain's Lineage; "sons of God" are from Seth's genealogy.

CHAPTER 5
- Jude 1:6 never states "Nephilim" or fallen angels went after "strange flesh."

CHAPTER 6
- 2 Peter never states fallen angels went after "strange flesh."

CHAPTER 7
- The Book of Enoch is fiction written thousands of years after Enoch left earth.

CONCLUSION
- The idea of demons mating with humans is satanic, not from God, and not in Scripture.

CONTENTS

CHAPTER 1: THE BIOLOGICAL, PHYSICAL & CREATIVE IMPOSSIBILITY OF FALLEN ANGELS REPRODUCING WITH HUMAN FEMALES............1

Biological Impossibility of Demon-Human Procreation	1
Only Human Sperm Can Penetrate a Human Egg	2
Physical Impossibility of Demon-Human Procreation	3
Demons/Fallen Angels Don't Have Bodies or DNA	3
Heavenly Realm v. Earthly Realm: Human Bodies and Celestial Bodies are Different	4
Fallen Angels Reserved in Chains of Darkness by God	5
Creative Impossibility of Demon-Human Reproduction	6
Satan Entered the Body of a Serpent	7
Satan Can Put Evil Thoughts into Men's Minds	9
Satan Can Occupy Existing Body	9
Demons Need to Possess Human Bodies	10
Nephilim Nonsense on GracethruFaith Website	12
Nonsense Refuted	14
What Jude Chapter 1 v. 6 Really Says	18
Conclusion to the Chapter	20
WORKS CITED & SCRIPTURE REFERENCED	21

CHAPTER 2: EVERY SCRIPTURE REFERENCE TO "SONS OF GOD" ALWAYS REFERS TO HUMANS, NOT FALLEN ANGELS..................22

At No Time Has God Called An Angel His Son	23
Scripture Says "Sons of God" are Believers, Not Fallen Angels	24
Luke's Genealogy of Jesus Shows "Sons of God" are Humans	26
Old Testament "Sons of God" Are From Seth's Lineage	28
Seth's Genealogy in Genesis Same as Jesus' in Luke's Gospel	28

Noah—One of the "Sons of God" in Seth's Line	30
Noah's "Righteousness" is Belief in God's Word	31
The Sons of God in Job are Reverent Men in Seth's Lineage	32
Job's "Sons of God" Same as Paul's and John's	33
Characteristics of the "Sons of God"	35
Sons of God in Genesis 6:2 and 6:4 are Human	36
Equating "Sons of God" with Fallen Angels Makes Jesus the Brother of Satan	38
Conclusion to the Chapter	39
SCRIPTURE REFERENCED	40

CHAPTER 3: OT "GIANTS" NOT HYBRIDS BUT INCLUDE ALL PRE-FLOOD HUMANS..41

Pre-Flood Giants Are All Human	42
"Men of Renown" Like Famous Men Today	43
Giants: Human Men of Large Stature	45
Post-Flood Giants are Human	45
Og, King of Bashan--Too Big for His Bed	46
Goliath, the 6'9" Philistine Lived After the Flood	47
Modern Giants are Human	48
No Demon DNA exists in Modern Humans	48
Nephilim Nonsense on RR Website	49
Nonsense Refuted	51
Conclusion to the Chapter	51
WORKS CITED & SCRIPTURE REFERENCED	53

CHAPTER 4: "DAUGHTERS OF MEN" ARE FROM CAIN'S LINEAGE AND "SONS OF GOD" ARE FROM SETH'S GENEALOGY...55

Antithetical Parallelisms: "Sons of God" from Seth; "Daughters of Men" from Cain	56
"Sons of God" in Old Testament	57
"Sons of God" in New Testament	58

Comparing/Contrasting Belief v. Unbelief and Genetic Lineage to Messiah/Jesus	59
Isaac Contrasted with Ishmael	59
Jacob Contrasted with Esau	60
The Birthright: From Seth's Genealogy in Genesis	60
Genesis Genealogy of Cain: "Daughters of Men"	61
Cain: a "Type" of the Lost/Judged	63
Genesis Genealogy of Seth: "Sons of God'	64
Reason for the Flood: Apostasy From Intermarriage of "Sons of God" with "Daughters of Men"	67
Tradition to Marry Inside the Faith/Lineage	70
The Theme: Believers Saved Out of Judgment	72
Redeeming Fallen Mankind Without Contravening Free Will	74
Conclusion to the Chapter	75
SCRIPTURE REFERENCED	76

CHAPTER 5: JUDE'S EPISTLE NEVER STATES THAT FALLEN ANGELS WENT AFTER "STRANGE FLESH".78

What Jude Chapter 1 Really Says	79
Jude Cautions Against Twisting Scripture	82
Nephilim Nonsense of Rapture Ready Website	83
Nonsense Refuted	85
RR Writer Says the Opposite Elsewhere	90
Conclusion to the Chapter	90
WORKS CITED & SCRIPTURE REFERENCED	92

CHAPTER 6: PETER'S 2ND EPISTLE NEVER STATES THAT FALLEN ANGELS WENT AFTER "STRANGE FLESH"..93

What 2 Peter Really Says	93
Angels Cast Down Involuntarily	94
Conclusion to the Chapter	96

CHAPTER 7: THE BOOK OF ENOCH IS NOT FACTUAL OR HISTORICAL..97	
Why The Book of Enoch is Not Canonical	97
Jesus Never Quoted the Book of Enoch	98
No Writer of Scripture Ever Quoted the Book of Enoch	98
Luke: Inspired by God	99
Paul: Inspired by the Holy Spirit	100
Jude: Directed by the Holy Spirit	101
Conclusion to the Chapter	101
CONCLUSION..104	
SCRIPTURE REFERENCED	107
SOURCES / REFERENCES..................................108	

CHAPTER 1: THE BIOLOGICAL, PHYSICAL & CREATIVE IMPOSSIBILITY OF FALLEN ANGELS REPRODUCING WITH HUMAN FEMALES

The Main False Premise of Nephilim Nonsense is that Demons/Fallen Angels Reproduced with Human Females because they were Capable of Becoming Human

Biological Impossibility of Demon-Human Procreation

Demon-human reproduction cannot have taken place. It is biologically impossible for anything other than the human male sperm to fertilize a human female oocyte, with the exception of the Holy Spirit in the case of the Lord Jesus. This is designed by God. For Christians to believe this they might as well believe in Evolution, although there has been found no missing link between fishes and birds, fishes and monkeys, platypuses and turtles, or camels producing dairy cows—much less humans.

Only Human Sperm Can Penetrate a Human Egg

In his fine work "Human Biology" a textbook that is used in top-tier universities, Michael D. Johnson MD explains:

"...for only one of several million sperm will fertilize the egg...for otherwise the zygote (fertilized cell) would end up with an abnormal number of chromosomes..."

Before fertilization the egg is surrounded by a protective covering called the zona pellucida and by a layer of cells derived from the follicle called the corona radiata. The tip of the sperm—which is called the acrosome—releases enzymes that digest a path for the sperm through the radiata to and through the zona pellucida into the egg's cell membrane.

When the first sperm makes contact with the cell membrane special protein 'keys' of the sperm recognize receptor protein 'locks' in the egg cell membrane, ensuring that only human sperm can penetrate a human egg."[1]

Physical Impossibility of Demon-Human Procreation

It is physically impossible for demons/fallen angels to reproduce with human females for many reasons: they don't have bodies or DNA because terrestrial and celestial bodies are different; the rebellious (fallen angels) of Jude 1 and 2 Peter are "reserved in chains of darkness" by God Himself.

Demons/Fallen Angels Don't Have Bodies or DNA

Angels—fallen or otherwise—don't have DNA. Fallen angels "left their first estate" [Jude 1], which means the heavenly realm. Just as if a person were to leave his or her first estate would mean that they moved out of their current residence to another habitation, perhaps a duplex across town. It does not mean that they miraculously turned into a coyote. When a fish breaks the surface of the water (its habitation) it does not miraculously turn into a duck.

Heavenly Realm v. Earthly Realm: Human Bodies and Celestial Bodies are Different

There is a big difference between earthly and heavenly (and formerly heavenly) bodies. In his work "The Book of Enoch EXPOSED!" Author David J. Steward states:

"Human Bodies and Celestial Bodies are Way Different. We also read in 1st Corinthians 15:39-40 All flesh is not the same flesh: but there is one kind of flesh of men, another flesh of beasts, another of fishes, and another of birds. There are also celestial bodies, and bodies terrestrial: but the glory of the celestial is one, and the glory of the terrestrial is another."

"[We can see from Scripture that]... celestial (heavenly) and terrestrial (earthly) are NOT compatible. Just as a fish cannot breed with a horse, or a cow with a whale, so cannot a fallen angel breed with a woman... (Matthew 22:30)" [2].

Fallen Angels Reserved in Chains of Darkness by God

Both Jude and Peter in their epistles state that the Lord God has reserved fallen angels in "chains of darkness":

Jude 1: 6: "And the angels which kept not their first estate, but left their own habitation, he hath reserved in everlasting chains under darkness unto the judgment of the great day."

2 Peter 2:4: "For if God spared not the angels that sinned, but cast them down to hell, and delivered them into chains of darkness, to be reserved unto judgment;"

Both Jude and Peter state these demons are being reserved for judgment. Jude states they are "in everlasting chains under darkness unto the judgment of that great day." The great day being the Day of the Lord, or the "time of Jacob's troubles" during the Tribulation, per Jeremiah 30:7:

> *"Alas! for that day is great, so that none is like it: it is even the time of Jacob's trouble; but he shall be saved out of it."*

These "chains of darkness" essentially mean "hell": the demons/fallen angels once had celestial bodies, but now they are disembodied. This is what happens when people die: they don't stop existing, yet either their bodies are cremated or they decompose after being buried. The ones who know Jesus Christ as their Lord and Savior are immediately with the Lord as the apostle Paul states in 2 Corinthians 5:8:

> *"We are confident, I say, and willing rather to be absent from the body, and to be present with the Lord."*

Creative Impossibility of Demon-Human Reproduction

The demons and Satan himself, do not possess the creative ability or power to fashion or manufacture human bodies for themselves. Only God can make a full grown human being.

The complexity and precision of the human body is masterfully designed by God, who personally fashioned Adam from the earth, and then personally fashioned Eve from Adam's side. Who then could abide the notion that Satan—who can't create but can only destroy—could fashion even one chromosome, much less a "human" body? However, if he did it would bring the Nephilim argument to a crashing halt, since he himself would be human and could not produce hybrids. However, we never read in Scripture that Satan or his minions become human or make human bodies for themselves. Only God has this creative power.

Satan Entered the Body of A Serpent

Even Satan, the chief fallen angel, cannot create/manufacture a human body. In fact Satan can't make anything, he only has the power (and mindset) to destroy. Genesis 3:1 states that Satan Entered the Body of a Serpent:

> *"Now the serpent was more subtle than any beast of the field which the LORD God had made. And h said unto the woman..."*

Satan's first tried and true tactic (and his second, third, fourth ...) is to get people to doubt the veracity of God's word, per Genesis 3:1-5:

> *"Yeah, hath God said, Ye shall not eat of every tree of the garden?....And the serpent said unto the woman 'Ye shall not surely die. For God doth know that in the day ye eat thereof, then your eyes shall be opened, and ye shall be as gods, knowing good and evil."*

Once people begin to doubt the straightforwardness of God's Word they go off on wild tangents—like Nephilim Nonsense Proponents.

From the Genesis narrative it can be seen that Satan's earthly body was that of a serpent at the time of getting Adam and Eve to doubt the veracity of God's word. It is evident here that Satan, the chief fallen angel, could not become human, nor could he manufacture a human body. He had to occupy the body of a creature.

Satan Can Put Evil Thoughts into Men's Minds. In John 13:2 it is shown that Satan put an evil thought into the heart (mindset) of Judas Iscariot to betray Jesus:

"And supper being ended, the devil having now put into the heart of Judas Iscariot...to betray him;"

Satan did not become human. He did not make a human body for himself. Therefore, if the "chief" fallen angel is incapable of becoming human, his lesser minions would also not be capable of doing so.

Satan Can Occupy an Existing Body. Satan can "occupy" a body, but he can't "become" a human. A case of Satan occupying an already existing human body is mentioned in Revelation Chapter 13 verse 3 as John writes:

"And I saw one of his heads as it were wounded to death; and his deadly wound was healed: and all the world wondered after the beast."

It is during this time of the Tribulation that the one-time friend of Israel—the diplomatic conqueror of Revelation Chapter 6:2 is revealed in Rev. 13:3-6 as the anti-Christ when he sets himself up in the Temple and claims himself to be God. Satan has taken control of this man's body and mindset—but Satan didn't create his body.

Demons Need to Possess Human Bodies

The Gospels show that demons can possess already existing bodies, but they cannot create or manufacture human bodies for themselves.

Following are Scripture references to demon possession in the New Testament:

Matthew 4:24 *"And his [Jesus'] fame went throughout all Syria: and they brought unto him all sick people that were taken with divers diseases and torments, and those which were possessed with devils, and those which were lunatick, and those that had the palsy; and he healed them."*

Matthew 8:16   "When the even was come, they brought unto him many that were possessed with devils: and he cast out the spirits with his word, and healed all that were sick:"

Matthew 8:28   "And when he was come to the other side into the country of the Gergesenes, there met him two possessed with devils, coming out of the tombs, exceeding fierce, so that no man might pass by that way."

Matthew 8:31   "So the devils besought him, saying, If thou cast us out, suffer us to go away into the herd of swine."

Matthew 8:33   "And they that kept them fled, and went their ways into the city, and told every thing, and what was befallen to the possessed of the devils."

Matthew 9:32   "As they went out, behold, they brought to him a dumb man possessed with a devil."

Matthew 9:33 "*And when the devil was cast out, the dumb spake: and the multitudes marvelled, saying, It was never so seen in Israel.*"

Matthew 17:18 "*And Jesus rebuked the devil; and he departed out of him: and the child was cured from that very hour.*"

From the above it can be ascertained that demons/fallen angels don't have bodies but in rare instances can occupy bodies of humans.

Nephilim Nonsense on GracethruFaith Website

GracethruFaith is a popular Christian website that many times provides good advice and interpretation of Scripture. However, when it comes to Nephilim Nonsense it is sometimes one of the chief offenders of "twisting Scripture."

One such example is given below. Afterward I refute the writer's false premises. I try to be gentle in doing so, but I must also make a strong case because people who hold themselves up as learned teachers and pastors on websites and other venues should not lead people astray with doctrines of demons.

Question from Reader: *"Q. Genesis 6:2 says "The sons of God saw the daughters of men that they were fair; and they took them wives of all which they chose." This may not be answerable but I would be interested in your thoughts on the following questions. I believe it's rightly taught that these "sons of God" are angels. Their union with the daughters of men produced the Nephilim or giant offspring. It appears that God created only male angels as there are no indications of any female angels identified in scripture. What would be the logic of creating males and no females for one thing. and why would these angels even have the ability to produce sperm. I know God does nothing without a very good reason."*

Answer from Grace thru Faith Website: *"A. God's logic in not creating female angels could be that there's no need for reproduction in the angelic ranks, since angels live forever. Jude 1:6 explains that the angels of Genesis 6 abandoned their natural origins (first estate). This means they took on human form which allowed them to mate with human women. This was a huge violation of God's*

Law for which they're still being held for judgment (2 Peter 2:4). If you're interested in this, I've written more on it in this article here. You can also stream or download our mp3 study on The Nephilim" [3].

Nonsense Refuted

False Premise: "God's logic in not creating female angels could be that there's no need for reproduction in the angelic ranks, since angels live forever."

Refute: Mankind was also made to live forever. This possibility was taken from them when sin entered the world.

Just because there is no reproduction in Heaven doesn't preclude God from making female angels. There are currently millions of females in Heaven along with males, and they do not reproduce because as Jesus pointed out in Matthew 22:30 they *"Neither marry nor are given in marriage."*

God doesn't even need male and female humans to reproduce as Jesus stated in Luke 3:8:

"God is able to from these stones raise children up to Abraham."

Perhaps God didn't make female angels because He was waiting to do his final opus in His act of creation—making the beautiful female.

False Premise: "Jude 1:6 explains that the angels of Genesis 6 abandoned their natural origins (first estate). This means they took on human form which allowed them to mate with human women."

Refute: There are no angels mentioned in Genesis 6. This is the story of mankind. As for the Scripture in 6:2:

"That the sons of God saw the daughters of men that they were fair; and the took them wives of all which they chose."

Scholarly Bibles in the King James Version always relate this verse to that of Deuteronomy 7:3,4:

"Neither shalt thou make marriages with them they daughter thou shalt not give unto his son, nor his daughter shalt thou take unto they son"

The above admonition to not marry with unbelievers is in context of Israel entering the Promised Land and having cast out several nations like the Hittites, Amorites, Canaanites, etc. (Intermarriage of believers with unbelievers, which brought about apostasy, which brought about the Noachian Flood, is discussed more in detail in Chapter 4).

In addition, leaving one's "first estate" does not mean demons became human. As mentioned earlier, if someone leaves their first estate it means they've moved to a new dwelling, not that they've morphed into a new type of creature. Again, a fish doesn't become a duck just because it breaks the surface of the water.

(Also, if fallen angels took on human form, then the whole argument of "demon-human" hybrids collapses, since demons would then be human, not hybrids: they would have human eyes, arms, ears, legs, sperm.... There can be no "hybrid" Nephilim from this.)

Scripture states that even Jesus Himself didn't just drop down from Heaven and become human (although I am sure He could have). He had to become a human (while remaining fully God) via the biological process, absent the human male sperm.

If demons could become human God would not have gone through the separate process of making fully formed humans in the persons of Adam and Eve.

It was God who made humans. Satan and his ilk do not have the knowledge, the skill, the capability to make humans, or craft themselves human bodies.

What Jude Chapter 1 v. 6 Really Says

Jude 1: 6: "And the angels which kept not their first estate, but left their own habitation, he hath reserved in everlasting chains under darkness unto the judgment of the great day."

The "first estate" the fallen angels left was Heaven. Because these angels rebelled against God, God has reserved them in chains of darkness as both Jude and Peter state in their epistles. Therefore, If God has reserved them in chains of everlasting darkness they could not have mated with human females.

"Chains of darkness" more than likely means they are disembodied. They can in spirit "roam the earth" like Satan, per 1 Peter 5:8:

"Be sober, be vigilant; because your adversary the devil, as a roaring lion, walketh about, seeking whom he may devour:"

In rare cases they can possess an already existing human body, but they cannot manufacturer human bodies for themselves, nor can they "turn human"/take on human form. Satan can, however, masquerade as an "angel of light," per Paul in 2 Corinthians 11:14:

"And no marvel; for Satan himself is transformed into an angel of light."

But the above is in the context of how Satan uses subtle deceit, such as twisting Scripture, or suggesting that Scripture is not true, or that God doesn't mean what He says, and that his satanic thoughts are brighter/better than God's:

Proverbs 14:12 "There is a way which seemeth right unto a man, but the end thereof are the ways of death."

1 John 5:19 "And we know that we are of God, and the whole world lieth in wickedness."

The above Scripture means that anything not of God is of Satan, who seems pretty sensible to the un-redeemed who don't have God's Holy Spirit and the wisdom God provides.

Conclusion to the Chapter

It has been shown that it is biologically, physically and creatively impossible for demon/fallen angels to have mated with human females to produce "Nephilim" or demon-human hybrid "giants."

Demons don't have bodies or DNA; they can't make themselves bodies or become human.

Genesis Chapter 6 does not speak of angels, fallen or otherwise: it is the story of mankind in the years prior to the Noachian Flood and shows how God dealt with the situation.

WORKS CITED & SCRIPTURE REFERENCED IN CHAPTER 1

[1] **Michael D. Johnson MD.** Human Biology Concepts and Current Issues. 5th Ed. Pearson Benjamin Cummings, San Francisco, CA. pp. 481-483.

[2] **David J. Stewart.** Human Bodies and Celestial Bodies are Way Different. The Book Of Enoch EXPOSED! November 2006.http://jesus-is-savior.com/Wolves/book_of_enoch.htm.

[3] **Nephilim Nonsense on GracethruFaith.** https://gracethrufaith.com/ask-a-bible-teacher/how-could-angels-do-this/Sunday, January 24th, 2016. Downloaded January 26th, 2016.

Rev. 6:2 …and behold a white horse: and he that sat on him had a bow; and a crown was given unto him: and he went forth conquering and to conquer,"

Rev. 13:3-6 And I saw one of his heads as it were wounded to death; and his deadly wound was healed: and all the world wondered after the beast. And they worshipped the dragon which gave power unto the beast: and they worshipped the beast, saying, Who is like unto the beast? who is able to make war with him? And there was given unto him a mouth speaking great things and blasphemies; and power was given unto him to continue forty and two months. And he opened his mouth in blasphemy against God, to blaspheme his name, and his tabernacle, and them that dwell in heaven.

CHAPTER 2: EVERY SCRIPTURE REFERENCE TO "SONS OF GOD" ALWAYS REFERS TO HUMANS, NOT FALLEN ANGELS

Nephilim Nonsense Promoters claim Fallen Angels are the "Sons of God" Mentioned in the Old Testament book of Job who Reproduced with "Daughters of Men" to Create Nephilim or "Giant" Demon-Human Hybrids

Nephilim Nonsense Promoters argue falsely that the "sons of God" in Scripture are fallen angels who "came into" (had sex with) "daughters of men" (humans) and thus produced demon-human hybrids they call Nephilim. However, God has never called an angel His "son" and every scripture reference in both the Old and New Testaments that speak of "sons of God" always refer to humans—not fallen angels.

At No Time Has God Called An Angel His Son

The apostle Paul in his epistle to the Hebrews 1:5 states:

"For unto which of the angels said he at any time, Thou art my Son…?"

The apostle Paul is not some nut running a website, bloviating on a blog, or selling books containing hype and nonsense. He is the great intellectual, the Hebrew of the Hebrews, who expounds on the meaning of the Old Testament and how it relates to the New Testament like no other apostle, disciple or anyone before or after him.

No human teacher touches Paul in terms of his breadth of knowledge and his inspiration from God's very Holy Spirit. Christians, then, should believe him when he declares:

"For unto which of the angels said he at any time, Thou art my Son"

This is a very plain statement and it doesn't take Biblical scholars to explain what it means.

Scripture Says "Sons of God" are Believers, Not Fallen Angels

In all of the following New Testament (NT) Scripture references "sons of God" or a version thereof is mentioned, and in all cases this refers to human beings who believe in Jesus—not to demons/fallen angels.

John 1:12 *"But as many as received him, to them gave he power to become the sons of God, even to them that believe on his name."*

Romans 8:14 *"For as many as are led by the Spirit of God, they are the sons of God."*

Romans 8:19 *"For the earnest expectation of the creature waiteth for the manifestation of the sons of God."*

Philippians 2:15 "That ye may be blameless and harmless, the sons of God, without rebuke, in the midst of a crooked and perverse nation, among whom ye shine as lights in the world;"

1 John 3:1 "Behold, what manner of love the Father hath bestowed upon us, that we should be called the sons of God: therefore the world knoweth us not, because it knew him not."

1 John 3:2 "Beloved, now are we the sons of God, and it doth not yet appear what we shall be: but we know that, when he shall appear, we shall be like him; for we shall see him as he is."

The aforementioned Scripture states that people who believe on the name of Jesus are sons of God; those led by the Holy Spirit are sons of God; those awaiting redemption are sons of God; the blames, harmless are sons of God; those beloved of God are sons of God; the sons of God will see Jesus in His Glory. That hardly sounds like demons/fallen angels.

Paul also writes in Hebrews 2:10 that Jesus, the Captain of the Christian faith who suffered on the cross, did so to bring *"many sons"*—human believers—into glory:

> *"For it became him, for whom are all things, and by whom are all things, in bringing many sons unto glory, to make the captain of their salvation perfect through sufferings."*

Luke's Genealogy of Jesus Shows "Sons of God" are Humans

Letting "Scripture interpret Scripture" is the most tried and true way of rightly dividing the Word of God. In Luke Chapter 3 the Holy Spirit calls men in Seth's lineage to Jesus "sons of God":

> *"22And the Holy Ghost descended in a bodily shape like a dove upon him, and a voice came from heaven, which said, Thou art my beloved Son; in thee I am well pleased.*
> *23 And Jesus himself began to be about thirty years of age, being (as was supposed) the son of Joseph, which was the son of Heli,*
> *24 Which was the son of Matthat, which was the son of Levi, which was the son of Melchi,*

which was the son of Janna, which was the son of Joseph,

25 Which was the son of Mattathias...

31 Which was the son of Melea, which was the son of Menan, which was the son of Mattatha, which was the son of Nathan, which was the son of David,

32 Which was the son of Jesse, which was the son of Obed, which was the son of Booz, which was the son of Salmon, which was the son of Naasson...

36 Which was the son of Cainan, which was the son of Arphaxad, which was the son of Sem, which was the son of Noe, which was the son of Lamech,

37 Which was the son of Mathusala, which was the son of Enoch, which was the son of Jared, which was the son of Maleleel, which was the son of Cainan,

38 Which was the son of Enos, which was the son of Seth, which was the son of Adam, which was the son of God."

Adam here is called "the son of God." He is clearly not a fallen angel. It is also important to note that while this genealogy goes back to Adam, it is his son Seth—not Cain—who is in the lineage of the Messiah/Jesus. This is significant, for later on and in Chapter 4 it will be shown that the "daughters of men"--whom Nonsense promoters argue are all human females--are in fact females in Cain's genealogy, while the "sons of God"--whom Nonsense promoters falsely claim are fallen angels--are in fact men in Seth's lineage.

Old Testament "Sons of God" Are From Seth's Lineage

God is consistent and changeless [James 1:17]. Jesus never changes [Hebrews 13:8]. If God would call "sons of God" in the New Testament the redeemed/believers who are beloved, blameless and harmless, He would not in the Old Testament call "sons of God" demons/fallen angels.

Seth's Genealogy in Genesis Same as Jesus' in Luke's Gospel

In Genesis Jesus' genealogy from Adam and Seth is similar to Luke's genealogy:

Gen. 4:25-26 "And Adam knew his wife again; and she bare a son, and called his name Seth: For God, said she, hath appointed me another seed instead of Abel, whom Cain slew.

26 And to Seth, to him also there was born a son; and he called his name Enos: then began men to call upon the name of the LORD." [Later on it is shown that this is what the book of Job in 1:6 and 2:1 references where it is said the "sons of God" presented themselves before the LORD.]

Gen. 5:1-32: "This is the book of the generations of Adam. In the day that God created man, in the likeness of God made he him; [Note here that God created man—meaning Satan can't drop down from Heaven—his "first estate"--and miraculously become human, nor can he create humans.]

2 Male and female created he them; and blessed them, and called their name Adam, in the day when they were created.

3 And Adam lived an hundred and thirty years, and begat a son in his own likeness, after his image; and called his name Seth:

4 And the days of Adam after he had begotten Seth were eight hundred years: and he begat sons and daughters...

21 And Enoch lived sixty and five years, and begat Methuselah:

22 And Enoch walked with God after he begat Methuselah three hundred years, and begat sons and daughters....and Enoch was not; for God took him....

28 And Lamech lived an hundred eighty and two years, and begat a son:

29 And he called his name Noah, saying, This same shall comfort us concerning our work and toil of our hands, because of the ground which the LORD hath cursed.

30 And Lamech lived after he begat Noah five hundred ninety and five years, and begat sons and daughters:

31 And all the days of Lamech were seven hundred seventy and seven years: and he died.

32 And Noah was five hundred years old: and Noah begat Shem, Ham, and Japheth."

Noah—One of the "Sons of God" in Seth's Line

Noah is one of the "sons of God" in Luke's genealogy of Jesus from Seth and Adam whom God directly calls His "son." Adam is not a demon-human hybrid.

This is another real blow to Nephilim Nonsense promoters because one of their fallacies is that God saved Noah because 1) he didn't give his daughters (he didn't have any) to demons/fallen angels whom Nonsense promoters call "sons of God" and/or 2) Noah's predecessors didn't give their daughters to demons.

First, Noah did not have any daughters. Secondly, Noah had no control over his predecessor's sex lives. Most importantly, "sons of God" does not refer to demons/fallen angels.

It is shown from the genealogies in Luke and in Genesis that Noah's predecessors are in Seth's lineage and they are the "sons of God" that Nephilim Nonsense promoters refer to as demons/fallen angels.

Noah's "Righteousness" is Belief in God's Word. Nonsense promoters claim Noah was righteous because his predecessors didn't give their daughters to demons/fallen angels (whom they erroneously refer to as "sons of God") so Noah "was born" of humans v. human-demon hybrids.

The last part is true: Noah is a human. From the genealogy in Luke and Genesis it can be determined that Noah was righteous in his generations from Seth's line of believers in God's promise of a Messiah from the seed of the woman. This means that Noah married a woman from Seth's lineage.

Scripture states that there is only one way to be "righteous" in God's eyes, and that stems from believing in what God has said or promised [Gen. 15:6; Galatians 3:6, et al]. This "righteousness" as it concerns Seth's lineage is the belief that God will send the Messiah through Seth, not Cain.

The Sons of God in Job are Reverent Men in Seth's Lineage

Job is thought by an overwhelming majority of Biblical scholars to be the oldest book in the Bible written by Moses. Moses is also the author of the first five books of the Bible: Genesis, Exodus,

Numbers, Deuteronomy and Leviticus. As such, Moses would not equate sons of God with demons or fallen angels.

It should be noted that the "sons of God" in Job are reverent/worshipful, as Scripture attests:

Job 1:6 "Now there was a day when the sons of God came to present themselves before the LORD, [showing reverence] *and Satan came also among them."*

Job 2:1 "Again there was a day when the sons of God came to present themselves before the LORD, and Satan came also among them to present himself before the LORD."

Job 38:7 "When the morning stars sang together, and all the sons of God shouted for joy?"

Job's "Sons of God" Same as Paul's and John's

In earlier pages of this Chapter it was shown that NT writers Paul and John called believers and followers of Jesus "sons of God":

John 1:12 *"But as many as received him, to them gave he power to become the sons of God, even to them that believe on his name."*

Romans 8:14 *"For as many as are led by the Spirit of God, they are the sons of God."*

Romans 8:19 *"For the earnest expectation of the creature waiteth for the manifestation of the sons of God."*

Since God is changeless, and His Holy Spirit inspired the Old and New Testament writers, these "sons of God" in Job are the believers in God's promise to send a Messiah. Job, then, is talking about men in Seth's lineage/genealogy. In Genesis 4:26 it is shown that men in Seth's genealogy called on the name of God:

"And to Seth, to him also there was born a son; and he called his name Enos: then began men to call upon the name of the LORD."

The phrase *"then began men to call upon the name of the LORD"* is what the book of Job is referencing in 1:6 and 2:1 where it is states that the "sons of God" presented themselves before God and Satan came with them. Calling on the name of God is what believers do, after all.

A telling point is the phrase "and Satan came with them." He is the chief fallen angel, but Moses, thought to be the writer of Job, does not call Satan a "son of God."

Couple the above evidence with the apostle Paul's statement that God never called an angel His son and the Nephilim argument crumbles further.

Characteristics of the "Sons of God"

Going back to what Paul and John wrote of sons of God, their characteristics can be enumerated:

- People who believe on the name of Jesus are sons of God;
- those led by the Holy Spirit are sons of God;
- those awaiting redemption are sons of God;

- the blames, harmless are sons of God;
- those beloved of God are sons of God;
- the sons of God will see Jesus in His Glory.

It is Jesus who makes people who believe in Him "sons of God" per Hebrews 2:10:

"For it became him, for whom are all things, and by whom are all things, in bringing many sons unto glory, to make the captain of their salvation perfect through sufferings."

Sons of God in Genesis 6:2 and 6:4 are Human

Nephilim Nonsense promoters are always looking to Genesis Chapter 6 as their basis for false teaching, like they pointed to Job's mention of "sons of God" saying they are fallen angels, when they have been shown not to be.

Scripture in Genesis Chapter 6 makes plain statements that to the sensible reader speak nothing of fallen angels or demons reproducing with human females.

Genesis 6:2 "That the sons of God saw the daughters of men that they were fair; and they took them wives of all which they chose."

Genesis 6:4 "There were giants in the earth in those days; and also after that, when the sons of God came in unto the daughters of men, and they bare children to them, the same became mighty men which were of old, men of renown."

From the above Scripture it is shown that "men" were the result of the union of the "sons of God" and "daughters of men"—not hybrids. That is because the "sons of God" are human men in Seth's lineage and the "daughters of men" are females in Cain's genealogy.

Luke's genealogy of Jesus says that all the men in Seth's lineage are the "sons of God." Therefore any mention of "sons of God" in Gen 6:2 and 6:4 can only be referring to human males, not demon-human hybrids.

Nonsense promoters claim that the phrase "mighty men" in Genesis 6:4 resulting from believers marrying unbelievers is evidence that

"Nephilim" were "giants" because of demon-human breeding. In Chapter 3 it will be shown that all pre-Flood humans were large, or "giants."

Equating "Sons of God" with Fallen Angels Makes Jesus the Brother of Satan

To equate "sons of God" with demons/fallen angels is to call the very Son of God-- Jesus --the brother of Satan and fallen angels. This is beyond absurdity and well into abject delusion.

Mormons believe that Jesus and Satan are brothers. "Christians" then who believe that "sons of God" are demons fall into the Mormon camp.

Jesus was pre-existent before Satan. In fact Scripture says He was the Word who spoke the world, universe and everything in them into existence [John 1:1-10].

Jesus said He saw Satan fall from Heaven [Luke 10:18].

Conclusion to the Chapter

It was shown using science and Scripture that it is biologically, physically and creatively impossible for demons/fallen angels to reproduce with human females. Demons don't have bodies or DNA, and they can't make themselves human bodies or become human.

The intellectual giant apostle Paul has stated that at no time did God call any angel His son. A big problem arises when people ignore Paul's statement and refer to "sons of God" as fallen angels because they are then elevating fallen angels to the status of the Lord Jesus, Who is The Son of God.

SCRIPTURE REFERENCED
IN CHAPTER 2

James 1:17   Every good gift and every perfect gift is from above, and cometh down from the Father of lights, with whom is no variableness, neither shadow of turning.

Hebrews 13:8   Jesus Christ the same yesterday, and to day, and for ever.

Genesis 15:6   And he believed in the LORD; and he counted it to him for righteousness.

Galatians 3:6   Even as Abraham believed God, and it was accounted to him for righteousness.

James 2:23   And the scripture was fulfilled which saith, Abraham believed God, and it was imputed unto him for righteousness: and he was called the Friend of God.

John 1:1-10   In the beginning was the Word, and the Word was with God, and the Word was God. The same was in the beginning with God. All things were made by him; and without him was not any thing made that was made. In him was life; and the life was the light of men. And the light shineth in darkness; and the darkness comprehended it not... He was in the world, and the world was made by him, and the world knew him not.

Luke 10:18   And he said unto them, I beheld Satan as lightning fall from heaven.

CHAPTER 3: "GIANTS IN THE EARTH" INCLUDES ALL PRE-FLOOD HUMANS

Nephilim Nonsense Promoters Claim that the "Giants" Referenced in Genesis Resulted From Demon-Human Reproduction

Nephilim Nonsense promoters point to Genesis 6:4 that states there were giants in the earth pre-Flood as a basis for their claim that "sons of God" were demons/fallen angels who procreated with human females:

"There were giants in the earth in those days;..."

Nonsense promoters don't take into consideration that everything was "giant" pre-Flood.

Pre-Flood Giants Are All Human

Everything was "giant" Pre-Flood, including humans, animals and vegetation. Creation scientists explain that because it never rained on the earth before the Flood [Genesis 2:5,6]; rather, a mist came up from the ground and Creation Scientists suspect there was a canopy of mist overhead in addition to more nitrogen in the atmosphere. Because of the canopy protection against the sun's harmful rays and the nitrogen everything—people, animals, plants—grew very large.

Because plants grew very lush and large is the reason for the large oil deposits/reserves on earth, especially in the Mesopotamian area, and off Israel's shores. Oil is not a fossil fuel, it is plant-based, and the earth long ago was covered in lush vegetation which was roiled and plowed under during the Noachian Flood.

The pre-Flood atmosphere is also the reason for giant reptiles we call Dinosaurs. Reptiles, unlike other species, keep growing throughout their lifespan. Some may be with us still as large lizards.

The atmosphere, or canopy, is also one of the reasons people grew very large, along with fact the early genetic makeup of mankind was purer, due to their DNA not having gone through as many replication cycles, and cells having not gone through as many meiotic / mitotic divisions. Plus, God had not yet set a limit on mankind's lifespan [Genesis 6:3]. Now this is an instance where there could be hideous chimeras today if God hadn't limited man's age span.

The Works Cited page at the end of this Chapter contains links to Creation science and other research on the subject of the Early Earth.

"Men of Renown" Like Famous Men Today

Nonsense promoters point to Scripture calling the offspring of early, genetically pure humans "men of renown" in an attempt to uphold their fallacy that demons mated with human females. But the phrase "men of renown" is a simple statement. Being "renown" means being well known. Sure, these large mean could probably lift really large things and maybe wrestle really big animals, but that doesn't mean they were demon-human hybrids.

Later on in this Chapter it is shown that the Israelites wiped out the last of the Rephaim giants, including their leader, Og, King of Bashan; and that David slew Goliath a 9-foot tall giant while David was still a young lad. This shows that "giants" were big indeed, but they were also human—not demon hybrids.

Men of renown in the OT were renown to humans of their day. Men of renown today are athletes, business tycoons, actors, military heroes, astronauts, etc. This does not mean they are demon-human hybrids.

As renowned as the men of the OT were to other men, they are not as renowned to God: those who perished in the flood are not named for posterity. After the flood the name Nimrod is mentioned, but never by the Lord in the same vein as Noah, Daniel, Moses, David, etc. Nimrod's renown is an example of men esteeming things that God doesn't think are worth anything [Luke 16:15].

Giants: Human Men of Large Stature. Another false premise propagated by Nephilim Nonsense promoters is that God sent the Noachian Flood to clear the earth of demon-human hybrid giants—the "men of renown" that Nonsense promoters claim are demon-human hybrids. Scripture doesn't say this. Scripture states that even after the Flood there were giants, per Genesis 6:4. This is due to pure human genetics.

Post-Flood Giants Are Human

Nonsense promoters fail to note that Gen. 6:4 also states:

"... <u>and also after that</u> [there were giants], when the sons of God came in unto the daughters of men, and they bare children to them, the same

became mighty men which were of old, men of renown."

This means that after the Flood there were giants in the human population.

Og King of Bashan—Too Big for His Bed.

In Deuteronomy Chapter 3 Scripture speaks of the Israelites wiping out one of the notable post-Flood giants, Og, King of Bashan, along with all his subjects:

1 "Then we turned, and went up the way to Bashan: and Og the king of Bashan came out against us, he and all his people, to battle at Edrei.

2 And the LORD said unto me, Fear him not: for I will deliver him, and all his people, and his land, into thy hand; and thou shalt do unto him as thou didst unto Sihon king of the Amorites, which dwelt at Heshbon.

3 So the LORD our God delivered into our hands Og also, the king of Bashan, and all his people: and we smote him until none was left to him remaining...

11 "For only Og king of Bashan remained of the remnant of giants; behold, his bedstead was a bedstead of iron; is it not in Rabbath of the children of Ammon? nine cubits was the length thereof, and four cubits the breadth of it, after the cubit of a man."

Og was a person, not a demon-human hybrid.

Goliath, the 6'9" Philistine Lived After the Flood

Many years after Og there was Goliath, a giant about 9 feet 9 inches tall. He is also a human male of large stature. He lived thousands of years after the Flood, as shown in 1 Samuel 17:4:

"And there went out a champion out of the camp of the Philistines, named Goliath, of Gath, whose height was six cubits and a span."

David slew this imposing genetic giant with a sling-shot, per 1 Samuel 17:49:

> *"And David put his hand in his bag, and took thence a stone, and slang it, and smote the Philistine in his forehead, that the stone sank into his forehead; and he fell upon his face to the earth."*

Modern Giants are Human

There are giant humans of modernity who suffer from "gigantism." In rare instances this disease produces people well in excess of 8 feet tall, and sometimes 9 feet tall. This is normally the result of too much growth hormone during childhood, probably because a tumor has developed on the thyroid. In rarer cases this is caused by a mutated gene [1].

No Demon DNA Exists in Human Genome

Research on the Human Genome has found no demon DNA. In the Works Cited page at the end of this Chapter links are provided to Christian and secular websites regarding this subject.

Nephilim Nonsense on Rapture Ready Website

Scripture states that God destroyed the world with the Flood and saved Noah, his wife, his three sons and their wives (8 people), plus the animals in the Ark. So if there were demon-human hybrids they would be wiped out. Because when God does something, He does it right. He doesn't make mistakes. But Nephilim Nonsense Promoters don't take God at His word (like those who perished in the Noachian Flood) and believe He didn't do a good job

Nonsense promoters teach that God did not wipe out all the unrighteous with the Flood. They claim that demon-hybrid DNA still persists in the human population because Gen. 6:4 also states *"...and also after that..."*

Following is Nonsense posted on Rapture Ready's (Christian) website:

"Hi, I was just watching [two Christian men, one of whom sells books about Nephilim] *discussing Nephilim and getting it totally wrong but then I thought this might be the reason for the giant Nephilim men and Nephilim Dinosaurs: The reason why the pre- and post-Flood Nephilim varies so greatly in size - pre were up to 300cubits - 450feet and working with the giant stones of Baalbeck would be no greater than a modern man working the stones typically used today - post were the 12/15/15 feet mentioned in post-Flood accounts - obviously at The Flood God bound all the fallen angels so they could not father any more giants - but their DNA was present in the blood of one of the wives of Noah's sons - but the Flood removed the protective canopy which had previously allowed gigantism in all things - 100ft dinosaurs, 300ft ferns etc and ensured that all the gigantism came to an end and toay we only see average sizes with the occasiaonal 'small' giant! The UFO cattle mutilations human abductions may definitely be the work of spirits of Satan getting tissue for hybridisation experiments" (sic)* [2].

Nonsense Refuted

This misguided soul, a fan of the aforementioned Christian website, believes that demon DNA exists in the human population. Even though Scripture never even broaches this subject and the fact it would be impossible for demons, who lack bodies, to have DNA. He has been led astray by Nephilim Nonsense promoters.

Conclusion to the Chapter

It was shown in Chapter 1 that it is biologically, physically and creatively impossible for demons/fallen angels to reproduce with human females: they don't have bodies or DNA; that God has at no time called an angel—fallen or otherwise—His son. In Chapter 2 it was shown that "sons of God" are believers/the redeemed in Luke's genealogy of Jesus, which are the same men in the Genesis genealogy of Seth.

In this Chapter it was shown that the pre-Flood "giants" were humans, like post-Flood and Modern Day "giants." As such, the fallacious arguments set forth by Nephilim Nonsense promoters fall apart.

The Lord Jesus commissioned His followers to spread the Gospel of Salvation and remission of sins, so that people can have a relationship with their Creator. That's what "teachers" on Christian websites need to focus on. The Lord said in Matthew 6:23:

"But if thine eye be evil, thy whole body shall be full of darkness. If therefore the light that is in thee be darkness, how great is that darkness!"

WORKS CITED & SCRIPTURE REFERENCED IN CHAPTER 3

[1] **Gigantism, Mosby's Medical Dictionary, 9th edition.** © 2009, Elsevier
http://medical-dictionary.thefreedictionary.com/gigantism
[jigan′ tizem] Etymology: L, gigas, giant. an abnormal condition characterized by excessive size and stature. It is caused most frequently by hypersecretion of growth hormone (GH) that occurs before the closure of the bone epiphyses; it occurs to a lesser degree in hypogonadism and in certain genetic disorders. Gigantism with normal body proportions and normal sexual development usually results from hypersecretion of GH in early childhood. Hypogonadism, by delaying puberty and closure of the epiphyses, may lead to gigantism. Excessive linear growth often occurs in males with more than one Y chromosome...

[2] **Nephilim Nonsense on RR Website**
"Interesting E-mail Both the pro and the con Jan4"
[http://www.raptureready.com/index.phpDownloaded/
http://www.raptureready.com/rap37.html.

Early Earth
Institute for Creation Research. http://www.icr.org/

Donald Wesley Patten. Catastrophism and the Old Testament The Mars-Earth Conflicts Pacific Meridian Pub Co; First Edition (September 1988)

Dr. Kent Hovind's website 2Peter3.com
https://2peter3.com/kent-hovind-canopy-theory-kjv-bible/

Genome Research
National Institute of Health (NIH) Human Genome Project (HGP) Research Institute
https://www.genome.gov/12011238

Institute for Creation Research. Numerous peer-reviewed scientific articles, several on Genome research. http://www.icr.org/

Genesis 2:5,6 ...for the LORD God had not caused it to rain upon the earth...But there went up a mist from the earth, and watered the whole face of the ground.

Genesis 6:3 And the LORD said, My spirit shall not always strive with man, for that he also is flesh: yet his days shall be an hundred and twenty years.

Luke 16:15 And he said unto them, Ye are they which justify yourselves before men; but God knoweth your hearts: for that which is highly esteemed among men is abomination in the sight of God.

CHAPTER 4: "DAUGHTERS OF MEN" ARE FROM CAIN'S LINEAGE AND "SONS OF GOD" ARE FROM SETH'S GENEALOGY

Nephilim Nonsense Promoters Claim the "Daughters of Men" in Genesis 6 are all Human Females and "Sons of God" are Demons/Fallen Angels

In this Chapter Scripture is compared with Scripture to show that the "daughters of men" are females in Cain's lineage, and that "sons of God" are human men in Seth's genealogy.

The phrases "daughters of men" and "sons of God" are broad antithetical parallelisms used to sharply contrast two types of people; that is believers with non-believers, in this case "sons of God" and "daughters of men." In addition, this Chapter shows that the intermarriage of believers with non-believers brought on apostasy whereby men's thoughts were evil continually and they filled the earth with violence, necessitating the judgment of the Flood.

Antithetical Parallelisms: "Sons of God" from Seth; "Daughters of Men" from Cain

Antithetical parallelism is a rhetorical device where the second line in verse or narrative expresses a sharp contrast to the first. These are used throughout Scripture especially in Hebrew poetic books. Thus use of antithetical parallelism is a Hebrew method of contrasting or showing wild gulfs between types of beliefs and behaviors.

The two phrases "sons of God" and "daughters of men" are used in the Old Testament as a type of broad v. rhetorical antithetical parallelism, since the Bible is overall all about Jesus, and Seth's lineage leads to Him. This can be illustrated by looking at the phrase "sons of God" as it is used in both the Old and New Testaments.

"Sons of God" in Old Testament

Genesis 6:2 *"That the sons of God saw the daughters of men that they were fair; and they took them wives of all which they chose."*

Genesis 6:4 *"There were giants in the earth in those days; and also after that, when the sons of God came in unto the daughters of men, and they bare children to them, the same became mighty men which were of old, men of renown."*

Job 1:6 *"Now there was a day when the sons of God came to present themselves before the LORD, and Satan came also among them."*

Job 2:1 *"Again there was a day when the sons of God came to present themselves before the LORD, and Satan came also among them to present himself before the LORD."*

Job 38:7 *"When the morning stars sang together, and all the sons of God shouted for joy?"*

From the OT it is shown in the book of Job—thought to be even older than Genesis—that the "sons of God" are at this early stage reverent or worshipful.

"Sons of God" in New Testament

John 1:12 "But as many as received him, to them gave he power to become the sons of God, even to them that believe on his name:"

Romans 8:14 "For as many as are led by the Spirit of God, they are the sons of God."

Romans 8:19 "For the earnest expectation of the creature waiteth for the manifestation of the sons of God."

Philippians 2:15 That ye may be blameless and harmless, the sons of God, without rebuke, in the midst of a crooked and perverse nation, among whom ye shine as lights in the world;"

1 John 3:1 "Behold, what manner of love the Father hath bestowed upon us, that we should be called the sons of God: therefore the world knoweth us not, because it knew him not.

1 John 3:2 "Beloved, now are we the sons of God, and it doth not yet appear what we shall be: but we know that, when he shall appear, we shall be like him; for we shall see him as he is."

It can be seen from the NT that believers/redeemed are the "sons of God" and they are all human.

Comparing/Contrasting Belief v. Unbelief and Genetic Lineage to Messiah/Jesus

The phrases "sons of God" and "daughters of men" is a contrasting of beliefs as it relates to the lineage/genealogy to Christ, which relates back to God's promise in Genesis to bring a Redeemer via the seed of a woman.

Examples of this "belief" v. "unbelief" as it relates to genealogy are Isaac and Ishmael, and Jacob and Esau. Isaac and Jacob are named in Jesus genealogy (from Seth), while Ishmael and Esau are not because they were non-believers or are symbolic of unbelief.

Isaac Contrasted with Ishmael

Isaac was the "son of the Promise" of God to send Messiah/Jesus from the seed of a woman through Seth's lineage from Abraham onward.

In contrast with Isaac, Ishmael was the son of un-belief or the flesh, meaning he is the result of mankind's own efforts. This element of unbelief/the flesh is inherent in Cain's rejected religious offering in Genesis Chapter 4:3-5:

> *"...that Cain brought of the fruit of the ground an offering unto the Lord. 4. And Abel, he also brought of the firstlings of his flock and of the fat thereof. And the Lord had respect unto Abel and to his offering: 5. But unto Cain and to his offering he had not respect."*

Jacob Contrasted with Esau

Jacob so wanted the birthright; that is, to be in the lineage to the Messiah/Jesus, that he first "purchased" it from Esau.

Esau so despised the birthright [Gen 17:19], which is the promise of God to send Messiah through Seth's lineage via Abraham that he easily sold it to Jacob for a bowl of soup. [Gen. 25:33].

The Birthright: From Seth's Genealogy in Genesis.

This birthright that Esau sold is shown in Genesis (and Luke) from Seth, the son of Adam who was called "son of God," to Noah "righteous in his generations" since he didn't marry outside the faith; to Shem...to Abraham...to Jacob who was later re-named Israel by God.

Genesis Genealogy of Cain: "Daughters of Men"

From Cain's lineage of "unbelief" come the "daughters of men." The following Scripture verses from Genesis Chapters 4 and 5 show Cain's lineage:

14 "Behold, thou hast driven me out this day from the face of the earth; and from thy face shall I be hid; and I shall be a fugitive and a vagabond in the earth; and it shall come to pass, that every one that findeth me shall slay me.
15 And the LORD said unto him, Therefore whosoever slayeth Cain, vengeance shall be taken on him sevenfold. And the LORD set a mark upon Cain, lest any finding him should kill him.
16 And Cain went out from the presence of the LORD, and dwelt in the land of Nod, on the east of Eden.

17 And Cain knew his wife; and she conceived, and bare Enoch: and he builded a city, and called the name of the city, after the name of his son, Enoch.

18 And unto Enoch was born Irad: and Irad begat Mehujael: and Mehujael begat Methusael: and Methusael begat Lamech….

22 And Zillah, she also bare Tubalcain, an instructer of every artificer in brass and iron: and the sister of Tubalcain was Naamah.

23 And Lamech said unto his wives, Adah and Zillah, Hear my voice; ye wives of Lamech, hearken unto my speech: for I have slain a man to my wounding, and a young man to my hurt.

24 If Cain shall be avenged sevenfold, truly Lamech seventy and sevenfold."

Cain's lineage is brief. He had no regard for the promises of God, as evidenced by his religious offering in Genesis 4:3-5 and his actions thereafter (killing his brother, naming a city after his first son, etc.); therefore, God seems to have had little motivation to go into detail of his lineage.

Cain: a "Type" of the Lost/Judged

Cain and his progeny are a "type" of "lost" or "judged. Types and figures are used thought Scripture. In Genesis Chapter 24 Abraham is a "type" or "pre-figure" of God the Father. Isaac is a type of Jesus as Abraham's son. Abraham's un-named Servant is a type of Holy Spirit who is commanded to find a bride, Rebekah (symbolic of the Church) for Abraham's son Isaac. He is instructed to not go outside the faith to the Canaanites.

This un-named Servant never testifies of Himself, but only of Isaac, just like the Holy Spirit never testifies of Himself, only about things of the Lord Jesus, as John 16:13-15 states:

"Howbeit when he, the Spirit of truth, is come, he will guide you into all truth: for he shall not speak of himself; but whatsoever he shall hear, [that] shall he speak: and he will shew you things to come. He shall glorify me: for he shall receive of mine, and shall shew [it] unto you. All things that

the Father hath are mine: therefore said I, that he shall take of mine, and shall shew [it] unto you."

Since Luke's Gospel calls all the men in Seth's lineage "sons of God"—due to their belief in God's promises, which is what made them "righteous" in God's eyes—then the "daughters of men" are from Cain's lineage of unbelief.

Genesis Genealogy of Seth: "Sons of God'

It was shown in Chapter 2 that God never called an angel—fallen or otherwise-- His "son." It was shown that the "sons of God" are reverent/worshipful men in Luke's genealogy of Jesus through Seth's line due to their belief in God's promise of a Messiah/Jesus via this birthright [James 2:23]. This belief is what makes people "righteous" in God's eyes—and what makes them "sons of God" per John and Paul:

John 1:12 "But as many as received him, to them gave he power to become the sons of God, even to them that believe on his name."

Romans 8:14 "For as many as are led by the Spirit of God, they are the sons of God."

Romans 8:19 "For the earnest expectation of the creature waiteth for the manifestation of the sons of God."

In Gen. 4 and 5 Seth's lineage is detailed like it is in Luke's Gospel:

Gen. 4:25-26 "And Adam knew his wife again; and she bare a son, and called his name Seth: For God, said she, hath appointed me another seed instead of Abel, whom Cain slew.
  26 And to Seth, to him also there was born a son; and he called his name Enos: then began men to call upon the name of the LORD." [This is what Job references where it is said the "sons of God" presented themselves and Satan came with them.*]*

Gen. 5:1-32: "This is the book of the generations of Adam. In the day that God created man, in the likeness of God made he him;

[Note in the above that God created man—meaning Satan can't drop down from Heaven—his "first estate" --and miraculously become human.]

2 Male and female created he them; and blessed them, and called their name Adam, in the day when they were created.

3 And Adam lived an hundred and thirty years, and begat a son in his own likeness, after his image; and called his name Seth:

4 And the days of Adam after he had begotten Seth were eight hundred years: and he begat sons and daughters…

21 And Enoch lived sixty and five years, and begat Methuselah:

22 And Enoch walked with God after he begat Methuselah three hundred years, and begat sons and daughters….and Enoch was not; for God took him….

28 And Lamech lived an hundred eighty and two years, and begat a son:

29 And he called his name Noah, saying, This same shall comfort us concerning our work and toil of our hands, because of the ground which the LORD hath cursed.

30 And Lamech lived after he begat Noah five hundred ninety and five years, and begat sons and daughters:

31 And all the days of Lamech were seven hundred seventy and seven years: and he died.

32 And Noah was five hundred years old: and Noah begat Shem, Ham, and Japheth."

It can be seen from the above that the males in Seth's lineage/genealogy are the "sons of God"—believers of God's promise to send a Messiah from Seth's lineage.

Reason for the Flood: Apostasy From Intermarriage of "Sons of God" with "Daughters of Men"

The apostasy and sinful behavior of mankind that brought God's judgment via the

Flood is a result of the intermarrying of believers with non-believers. That is, the intermarriage of the "sons of God" from Seth's lineage with the "daughters of men" in Cain's lineage.

Many times in Scripture God warns believers not to marry unbelievers [Nehemiah 13:23, etc.]. Paul in 2 Corinthians 6:14 cautions Christians to not become unequally yoked with unbelievers:

> *"Be ye not unequally yoked together with unbelievers: for what fellowship hath righteousness with unrighteousness? and what communion hath light with darkness?"*

In Chapter 1 it was shown that scholarly Bibles cross-reference Genesis 6 (which speaks of sons of God marrying daughters of men) to the admonition in Deuteronomy 7:3 against marrying outside the faith. Deuteronomy 7:3 is then cross-referenced to Joshua 23:12 which states:

> *"Else if ye do in any wise go back, and cleave unto the remnant of these nations, even*

these that remain among you, and shall make marriages with them, and go in unto them, and they to you: Know for certainty that the LORD your God will no more drive out any of these nations from before you; but they shall be snares and traps unto you, and scourges in your sides, and thorns in your eyes, until ye perish from off this good land which the LORD your God hath given you."

Additionally, Deuteronomy 7:3 is also cross-referenced with 1 Kings 11:2:

"Of the nations concerning which the LORD said unto the children of Israel, Ye shall not go in to them, neither shall they come in unto you: for surely they will turn away your heart after their gods...."

This marrying of believers with non-believers is an unfortunate theme throughout Scripture. The result of this at best is lukewarm worship, and at worst denigrates to all-out apostasy, which can be seen from the Genesis narrative as the reason God sent the Flood.

Nephilim Nonsense Promoters erroneously claim that the reason God sent the Flood is because the "sons of God"—allegedly demons—had sex with human females. This was shown to be false. It has also been show that demons cannot make human bodies or become humans, or mate with humans.

The reason God sent the Flood is apostasy, whereby the thoughts of mankind were evil continually, per Genesis 6:5:

"And God saw that the wickedness of man was great in the earth, and that every imagination of the thoughts of his heart was only evil continually."

An evil imagination is one that holds the Nephilim Nonsense doctrine.

Tradition to Marry Inside the Faith/Lineage

Many instances in Scripture show that people marry into their own lineage, or at least not outside their faith. Earlier it was stated that Abraham commanded his Servant not to search outside Israel amongst the unbelieving Canaanites for a wife for his son Isaac. Close marriage with near kin was permissible still at this time—and especially during Noah's time—because the human genome was not as degraded as it is today.

A few chapters later in Genesis we read that Esau have sold his birthright—that is, to be in the lineage of the Messiah/Jesus. Esau then again shows his disdain for God's promise of a Messiah by marrying outside the tribes of Israel, per Genesis 26:34:

> *"And Esau was forty years old when he took to wife Judith the daughter of Beeri the Hittite, and Bashemath the daughter of Elon the Hittite:"*

In this case Esau was acting exactly as Cain had acted, and as the "sons of God" eventually acted when they married into Cain's lineage. Cain disregarded God's promise as shown by his fleshy sacrifice [Gen. 4:3-5] and his sons took many wives. As time went by men from Seth's line married into Cain's lineage. They became lukewarm believers, corrupted by unbelievers, then out right apostates with only evil thoughts continually and filled the earth with violence. That is what Scripture tells us. It does not say that because demon-human hybrids popped up God sent the Flood.

The "sons of God" who married the "daughters of men" in Cain's lineage left their beliefs, were not humble or God-fearing like Noah. Thus, they scoffed at Noah's warning and were destroyed by the Flood. This destruction of apostates is consistent in Scripture.

The Theme: Believers Saved Out of Judgment

Just as the destruction of non-believers is a theme throughout Scripture, another even more compelling theme running throughout Scripture is

God's preserving or saving believers from judgment.

Scripture contains many instances of individuals saved out of judgment because of their belief in the Hebrew God/Jesus. There are way too many instances of this to mention all here, but in Genesis it was first Enoch (the first person raptured) [Gen. 5:24], then Noah and his family, then Lot and his daughters in Genesis 19. In Exodus God saved the Hebrew nation while destroying the unbelieving Egyptians. In Joshua 6:23 Rahab and her family were saved from judgment because of Rahab's belief in the mighty Hebrew God.

All those saved from judgment were "righteous" because of their belief in God. Noah was righteous in that he believed God would send Messiah through Seth's lineage. Noah is one of the "sons of God" mentioned in Luke's genealogy of Jesus.

Redeeming Fallen Mankind Without Contravening Free Will

A sincere Bible reader will note that the gist of the Bible is God's effort to redeem fallen mankind without contravening our free will. Scripture is about the promised Messiah—Jesus-- not Nephilim. On this point is where Satan has twisted the mindset of certain Christians who propagate Nephilim Nonsense as they miss the point of the whole Genesis narrative.

In Genesis we learn that Eve had Cain, then Abel. Cain, and his progeny symbolize Unbelief and disregard for God's promises. Cain slew Abel and was banished [Gen. 4:8; 4:16]. Eve then had Seth, and her attitude changed, knowing that God Himself will go through with His promise of a Messiah regardless of human effort to make or even try to prevent this from happening. From Seth's line we get Jesus, the Savior, the Messiah.

Conclusion to the Chapter

It was shown in this Chapter that Genesis contrasts believers in God's promise to send a Messiah/Jesus from the seed of a woman through Seth's lineage ("sons of God") with Cain's lineage of unbelief/disregard, hence the antithetical term "daughters of men."

Genesis Chapter 6 is the story of two types of people: believers and unbelievers. Noah believed God's promise of a Savior, while Cain from the very beginning did not believe God or regard His precepts. Noah's beliefs—and his resulting actions/behavior--were the opposite of apostates. And that is the point of the Genesis narrative.

SCRIPTURE REFERENCED IN CHAPTER 4

Genesis 17:19 Genesis 17:19 And God said, Sarah thy wife shall bear thee a son indeed; and thou shalt call his name Isaac: and I will establish my covenant with him for an everlasting covenant, and with his seed after him

Genesis 25:33 And Jacob said, Swear to me this day; and he sware unto him: and he sold his birthright unto Jacob.

James 2:23 And the scripture was fulfilled which saith, Abraham believed God, and it was imputed unto him for righteousness: and he was called the Friend of God.

Nehemiah 13:23 In those days also saw I Jews that had married wives of Ashdod, of Ammon, and of Moab...

Genesis 4:3-5 "...that Cain brought of the fruit of the ground an offering unto the Lord. 4. And Abel, he also brought of the firstlings of his flock and of the fat thereof. And the Lord had respect unto Abel and to his offering: 5. But unto Cain and to his offering he had not respect.

Gen. 5:24 "And Enoch walked with God: and he was not; for God took him."

Genesis 19:15 And when the morning arose, then the angels hastened Lot, saying, Arise, take they wife and thy two daughters, which are here; lest thou be consumed in the iniquity of the city.

Joshua 6:23 And the young men that were spies went in, and brought out Rahab, and her father, and her mother, and her brethren, and all that she had; and they brought out all her kindred, and left them without the camp of Israel.

Gen. 4:8 …and it came to pass, when they were in the field, that Cain rose up against Abel his brother, and slew him.

Gen. 4:16 And Cain went out from the presence of the LORD, and went in the land of Nod, on the east of Eden.

CHAPTER 5: JUDE's EPISTLE NEVER STATES THAT FALLEN ANGELS "WENT AFTER STRANGE FLESH"

Nephilim Nonsense Promoters Point to Jude's Epistle to Uphold the False Premise that Fallen Angels "Went After" Strange Flesh"

Nephilim Nonsense promoters in trying to prove demons mated with human females quote Jude Chapter 1 out of context, putting v. 6 after v. 7. This makes it appear that Jude talks about Nephilim/fallen angels going after "strange flesh."

When these verses are taken out of order and out of context it appears that Jude first speaks of men of Sodom and Gomorrah going after strange flesh then speaks of angels who did not keep their first estate "in like manner" went "after strange flesh." But this isn't what Jude writes at all.

What Jude Chapter 1 Really Says

This is a repeated heading and discussion but these bear repeating because of their importance in refuting the faulty logic of Nephilim Nonsense promoters. Jude Chapter 1 in fact states quite the opposite of what Nonsense Promoters claim. Also, this epistle is a scathing indictment of people who would twist Scripture.

v.4 "For there are certain men crept in unawares, who were before of old ordained to this condemnation, ungodly men, turning the grace of our God into lasciviousness, and denying the only Lord God, and our Lord Jesus Christ.
v. 5 I will therefore put you in remembrance, though ye once knew this, how that the Lord, having saved the people out of the land of Egypt, afterward destroyed them that believed not."

Verse 4 is about ungodly people who have turned the grace of God into lasciviousness. Even before the present time Jude is saying that God in the far past ordained these types of people into condemnation—that is if they kept it up and didn't repent. This does not speak of fallen angels.

Verse 5 is about people who were destroyed after God saved them out of Egypt. This has nothing to do with pre-Flood events. After being set free from Egypt many Israelites who didn't believe God were destroyed, and others languished in unbelief and died before entering the Promised Land. This is consistent throughout Scripture: after much patience and pleading with people to repent, God is left with no choice but to destroy the wicked. The main reason for this is because unbelievers corrupt believers.

v. 6 "And the angels which kept not their first estate, but left their own habitation, he hath reserved in everlasting chains under darkness unto the judgment of the great day."

Here in verse 6 Jude states that the "first estate" the angels left was Heaven--their "habitation." This does not mean that after they left they took on a different physical structure.

This verse also states that God has reserved these angels in chains under darkness. This means they are without bodies, which means they certainly cannot have mated with human females.

The important thing to note from v. 6 is that it never states that fallen/rebellious angels ever went after human females or "went after" "strange flesh" as Nephilim Nonsense promoters argue. This verse also never states that the fallen angels acted lasciviously.

v.7 "Even as Sodom and Gomorrah, and the cities about them in like manner, giving themselves over to fornication, and going after strange flesh, are set forth for an example, suffering the vengeance of eternal fire."

In verse 7, Jude speaks of a whole new class of peoples—not fallen angels, and not the people in v. 5 who left Egypt and then perished because of unbelief. The phrase "in like manner" refers to the behavior of the men in the cities round about Sodom and Gomorrah and who afterward would engage in the same behavior. This verse speaks of men, not fallen angels.

Jude Cautions Against Twisting Scripture

v.8 "Likewise also these filthy dreamers defile the flesh, despise dominion, and speak evil of dignities."

When people say that fallen angels mated with human females they denigrate women who are made in God's very image, pre Genesis 1:27:

"So God created man in his own image, in the image of God created he him; male and female created he them."

Plus, they are speaking things they know nothing about. The next verse is a serious warning against this.

v.10 "But these speak evil of those things which they know not: but what they know naturally, as brute beasts, in those things they corrupt themselves."

Proponents of demon-human mating seem incapable of higher reasoning or understanding human biology as God designed it.

v.11 "Woe unto them! for they have gone in the way of Cain (unbelief), and ran greedily after the error of Balaam for reward..."(preaching falsely for profit).

Preachers, websites and others that have perpetuated the pornographic idea of demons mating with human females seem to have done so to attract follows and to sell books on the subject.

Nephilim Nonsense of Rapture Ready Website

Like Grace through Faith Rapture Ready is a popular Christian website. Many times thoughtful Christians post helpful articles; however, more often than not self-described "teachers" post write-ups that are less than edifying, to put it mildly.

One such example is given below. Afterward I refute the writer's false premises. Again, I try to be gentle in doing so, but I must also make a strong case because people who hold themselves up as learned teachers and pastors on websites and other venues should not lead people astray with doctrines of demons.

The following write-up "Strange Flesh Punishment—God Style" is by the late Ron Graham:

> "...Do you sense, as I do, that God was thoroughly put out with His creation? Is it possible that God could become so angry that He would, once again, destroy the earth and everything on it? In Matthew's Gospel, Jesus tells four of His disciples that in the last days just before His return, earth's inhabitants will experience the same evil as they did prior to the flood of Noah. What did that evil consist of? It was a time filled with angels and humans going after "strange flesh"(sic) [1].

Nonsense Refuted

Refute. Graham mixes up pre-Flood people: Sodom and Gomorrah were post--Flood and the "strange flesh" refers to the men of these cities having sex with other men.

Graham goes on to twist things further:

"The word of God never fails to enlighten no matter how many times we read it. I was astonished at a verse I read recently, one I had read many times in the past, but this time a little nugget took hold and really sunk in. It speaks of God's punishment. "And the angels which kept not their first estate, but left their own habitation, he hath reserved in everlasting chains under darkness unto the judgment of the great day."

"Jude 1:6. Jude is referring to the fallen angels of Genesis 6 that co-habituated with human women. They had to leave their first estate, their own habitation, when they took on a form that would allow them to indulge in sexual relations with human women (they were going after strange flesh). "That the sons of God saw the

daughters of men that they were fair; and they took them wives of all which they chose." Genesis 6:2. Sons of God, or "Ben Ha Elohiym" in the original Hebrew text of the Old Testament, always refers to angels."

False Premise: Ron says "Jude is referring to the fallen angels of Genesis 6 that co-habituated with human women."

Refute: Nowhere in Jude or all of Scripture do we find evidence for this. Jude doesn't say this at all. This is merely from the mind of a man who is confused. Jude 1:6 says "And the angels which kept not their first estate, but left their own habitation, he hath reserved in everlasting chains under darkness unto the judgment of the great day."

False Premise: Ron then states that fallen angels "… had to leave their first estate, their own habitation, when they took on a form that would allow them to indulge in sexual relations with human women (they were going after strange flesh)."

Refute: Fallen angels were cast out of heaven by God, meaning they didn't go willingly. As for Ron's statement that they "had to in order to take on a different form": Nowhere does Scripture uphold this false belief. As for Ron's calling human women "strange flesh"; he is unmindful that women are made in the very image of God.

False Premise: Ron says of fallen angels "They had to leave their first estate, their own habitation, when they took on a form that would allow them to indulge in sexual relations with human women (they were going after strange flesh)."

Refute: Ron repeats himself, doesn't get it that God himself cast out the fallen angels. Also, again he provides no Scriptural evidence that fallen angels took on a "form that would allow them to indulge in sexual relations with human women." A statement merely from a man's imagination is not evidence for anything. That is like an "artists rendition" of what the earth looked like "millions of years ago" in a textbook that teaches Evolution.

As far as leaving one's "habitation": again, habitation and estate mean dwelling place, not a different bodily structure.

False Premise: Ron says "Genesis 6:2. Sons of God, or "Ben Ha Elohiym" in the original Hebrew text of the Old Testament, always refers to angels."

Refute: Does it really? Ron is just repeating what he has heard others say. "Ben" does mean "son." "Ha Elohiym" means "of God." Jesus was thought to be "Messiah ben Joseph"—meaning the son of Joseph, as a "suffering Servant" during his first Advent; and "Messiah ben David"—meaning the son of David, as a conquering King in His second Advent.

Scripture shows that "sons of God" refers to males in Seth's lineage. In numerous other areas

Scripture consistently shows that "sons of God" are believers. Jesus is the Son of God. To equate Him with an angel, fallen or otherwise, is lunacy.

False Premise: Ron goes on to say "Then Jude goes on and describes another set of events where God, once again used the most extreme of punishments to eliminate a people who had gone way past God's ordained and well established normal marital relations by going after "strange flesh. "Even as Sodom and Gomorrah, and the cities about them in like manner, …"

Refute: Nowhere in the Genesis pre-Flood narrative does it say that fallen angels went after "strange flesh." Ron is merely repeating what he has heard others say. The men of Sodom and Gomorrah and the cities round about them went after "strange flesh"; that is, human males had sex with other human males.

RR Writer Says the Opposite Elsewhere

In another of Ron Graham's archived posts on RR entitled "The Gadarene Demoniac" he contradicts what he said in the above write-up:

"Demons must seek embodiment, because for a demon to be without a body to inhabit places them in idleness which is the same for them as being in Hell" [2].

Here Graham is correct: demons (fallen angels) need to possess people. They cannot just take on human form or "become" human.

Conclusion to the Chapter

Jude never writes that fallen angels "went after strange flesh." He writes that these rebellious angels are reserved in chains of darkness until judgment.

Since Scripture is spiritually discerned [1 Corinthians 2:14] one must have wisdom from God's Holy Spirit to rightly divide the word of God and not have the term "Christian" become a laughing stock as happens when people talk Nonsense about demon-human mating/reproduction.

WORKS CITED & SCRIPTURE REFERENCED IN CHAPTER 5

[1] **Nephilim Nonsense on Rapture Ready**
Strange Flesh Punishment – God Style, By Ron Graham
Archived on Rapture Ready
http://www.raptureready.com/featured/graham/g147.html.
Downloaded verbatim January 26th 2016.

[2] "The Gadarene Demoniac"
http://www.raptureready.com/featured/graham/g54.html
Downloaded verbatim Jan 26th, 2016.

1 Cor. 2:14 But the natural man receiveth not the things of the Spirit of God: for they are foolishness unto him: neither can he know them, because they are spiritually discerned.

CHAPTER 6: 2 PETER NEVER MENTIONS FALLEN ANGELS WENT AFTER "STRANGE FLESH"

Nephilim Nonsense Promoters Point to Peter's 2nd Epistle to Uphold Their False Teaching that Nephilim/Fallen Angels Allegedly became Human to Go After "Strange Flesh"

Nephilim Nonsense promoters twist Scripture in 2 Peter Chapter 2 the same way the twist verses and phrases in Jude's epistle: they reverse the order of the verses and take the statements out of context.

What 2 Peter Really Says

In 2 Peter 2:4 onward he speaks of God not sparing the angels, then speaks of God judging the world with the flood, then speaks of the judgment of Sodom and Gomorrah. This is in the same order as Jude, and like Jude Peter speaks of separate incidents/judgments.

v. 4 "For if God spared not the angels that sinned, but cast them down to hell, and delivered them into chains of darkness, to be reserved unto judgment;"

Angels Cast Down Involuntarily

These angels were *cast down* from their first estate, which was Heaven. They did not go willingly to "become human" as Nephilim Nonsense promoters teach. Also, it is clear that these fallen angels are in hell (delivered into chains of darkness) and do not have bodies; thus, they cannot procreate with human females.

v. 5 "And spared not the old world, but saved Noah the eighth person, a preacher of righteousness, bringing in the flood upon the world of the ungodly;

v. 6 "And turning the cities of Sodom and Gomorrah into ashes condemned them with an overthrow, making them an ensample unto those that <u>after</u> should live ungodly..."

Peter places verses 5 and 6 in the same order as Jude, except Peter puts more space (period of time) between the two separate, unrelated judgments.

In v. 5 Peter says that Noah was a preacher of righteousness. Righteousness is about believing God.

In v. 6 Peter, like Jude, is warning people who would <u>*after the overthrow*</u> of Sodom and Gomorrah act like the men of those cities. It does not refer to Nephilim/fallen angels allegedly "going after strange flesh."

v. 7 "And delivered just Lot, vexed with the filthy conversation of the wicked:"

Peter here states that Lot was saved from judgment which fell upon the wicked inhabitants of Sodom and Gomorrah. In this manner, Lot is like

Noah: saved out of judgment because he believed in the Hebrew God and lived accordingly.

Conclusion to the Chapter

Peter never states that fallen angels "went after strange flesh." He states that rebellious angels were cast out of Heaven by God—that they didn't go willingly to "become human" as Nephilim Nonsense promoters claim. Peter says that these angels were delivered into chains of darkness "to be reserved unto judgment."

CHAPTER 7: THE BOOK OF ENOCH ISN'T GOD-BREATHED

Nephilim Nonsense Promoters Believe the Book of Enoch is God-Breathed and They Derive Much of Their Nonsense about Nephilim From It

Nephilim Nonsense promoters, in addition to twisting Scripture (which is what Satan himself does), refer to fanciful extra Biblical literature to uphold their false teaching. The Book of Enoch is once such source that Nonsense promoters elevate to the same status as Scripture. Nonsense promoters falsely claim that Jesus, Luke, Jude and Paul quoted from it.

Why The Book of Enoch is Not Canonical

The book of Enoch is not canonical because it was written thousands of years after Enoch walked the earth (about 200 years after Christ) and the writer could not have been witness to the events described in it. Additionally, scholars note there are many theological inconsistencies within the work. This book is categorized as *Pseudographa* meaning "false title" because it was written by a person other than whose name is attached to it.

Jesus Never Quoted the Book of Enoch

Jesus never quoted the book of Enoch. An online search of the King James Bible at http://www.kingjamesbibleonline.org/ and at http://Biblehub.net will not turn up one instance of Jesus quoting this book. A thorough reading of the NT will not turn up one instance of Jesus quoting this book.

No Writer of Scripture Ever Quoted the Book of Enoch

It bears repeating that the book of Enoch was written by an author whose name is more than likely not the same name as in the title.

Whatsmore, it was penned thousands of years after Enoch walked the earth.

But misguided Nonsense promoters claim that Luke 3:37 and Hebrews11:15 are instances where the book of Enoch is "quoted," and that Jude in 1:14 quotes from it. This is not the case at all: both Luke and Paul refer to Scripture in Genesis and they along with Jude were inspired to write what they did by God's Holy Spirit.

Luke: Inspired by God

In what Chapter in the following verses it can be seen that Luke quotes Genesis or is really just inspired by the Holy Spirit to write this.

v. 37 "Which was the son of Mathusala, which was the son of Enoch, which was the son of Jared, which was the son of Maleleel, which was the son of Cainan,
v. 38 Which was the son of Enos, which was the son of Seth, which was the son of Adam, which was the son of God."

Paul: Inspired by the Holy Spirit

Paul in Hebrews 11:5 refers to Genesis, and from inspiration of the Holy Spirit he explains why God raptured Enoch:

"By faith Enoch was translated that he should not see death; and was not found, because God had translated him: for before his translation he had this testimony, that he pleased God."

What could it mean that Enoch "pleased God"? It is not that his predecessors didn't give his daughters to marry demons, for Enoch would have no personal control over whether this happened or not. Pleasing God is what Abel did in his sacrifice, bringing God the best lamb from his flock to confirm his belief that God would send a Savior (His own Lamb) to redeem fallen mankind. Enoch was likely one of the "sons of God" in Job who began to "call upon the name of God."

None of this is about demon-human reproduction.

God is consistent and doesn't require one type of righteousness in the OT and another type of righteousness in the NT. Enoch pleased God in that he believed God and lived accordingly; he didn't live accordingly to find favor with God.

Jude: Directed by the Holy Spirit

Jude was directed by The Holy Spirit to quote Enoch himself, a "son of God" in the lineage of Seth. This is not the same as "quoting the Book of Enoch." Here's what the Holy Spirit instructed Jude to write in 1:14:

"And Enoch also, the seventh from Adam, prophesied of these, saying, Behold, the Lord cometh with ten thousands of his saints."

Conclusion To The Chapter

What has happened in the minds of Nephilim Nonsense promoters is that they have left off common sense, in addition to veering dangerously far from the faith, as the apostle Paul wrote in 1 Timothy 4:1:

"Now the Spirit speaketh expressly, that in the latter times some shall depart from the faith, giving heed to seducing spirits, and doctrines of devils;"

Nephilim Nonsense promoters evidently can't conceive of the fact that the pseudo writer of the book of Enoch—written thousands of years after Enoch walked the earth—had been reading Scripture and formulated a fanciful narrative around the bits and pieces he selected out of God's word. In contrast, writers of Scripture were inspired by God's Holy Spirit to write what they did, which always points to the Lord Jesus—not Nephilim—per the apostle Peter in 2 Peter 1:16:

"For we have not followed cunningly devised fables, when we made known unto you the power and coming of our Lord Jesus Christ, but were eyewitnesses of his majesty."

Paul warns in 2 Timothy 4:4:

"And they shall turn away their ears from the truth, and shall be turned unto fables."

Hopefully, this book can help remedy that trend and be used to turn people back to truth, or help make sure people don't stray from it in the first place.

CONCLUSION

The idea of demons reproducing with human females is satanic.

- It is biologically, physically and creatively impossible for demons/fallen angels, who lack bodies much less DNA, to reproduce with human females. Scripture states that disembodied demons/fallen angels must occupy existing bodies.

- The apostle Paul states that at no time has God called an angel his son. If God has not called an un-fallen angel His son, He sure wouldn't refer to a fallen angel as His son.

- "Sons of God" are believers in the Redeemer—Jesus—and are in Seth's genealogy in Luke's Gospel and in Genesis. Since "sons of God" are from Seth's genealogy, the "daughters of men" are from Cain's genealogy.

- The book of Job mentions the sons of God as reverent who presented themselves before God, as believers are apt to do. Job records that "Satan came with them." Satan, the chief fallen angel cannot be a "son of God" since that would mean he is the brother of the Lord Jesus.

- After generations certain "sons of God"—Seth's lineage—married un-believers from Cain's lineage, and gradually became apostate where their thoughts were evil continually and they did violence to their fellow humans; therefore God sent the Flood.

- Noah, from Seth's lineage, did not marry a woman from Cain's lineage; did not forget God's promises and believed God, so God accounted his belief as "righteousness" just as God did with Abraham [James 2:23].

- Nephilim Nonsense Promoters misquote Jude 1:6 and 2 Peter. Neither apostle states that fallen angels "went after strange flesh" but both say God has reserved fallen angels "in chains of darkness…," which means they are disembodied.

- The book of Enoch is non-canonical because it was written by someone other than whose name is in the title thousands of years after Enoch lived. Also, no writer of canonical Scripture ever quoted The Book of Enoch.

- Christians who perpetuate the nonsense that Nephilim are demon-human hybrids give people an inaccurate image of a loving God and thus "Profane the name of God" to the nations [Romans 2:24].

It is OK to make mistakes. Nobody is perfect. But God warns people about the serious consequences of twisting His Word on purpose [Revelation 21:27] and leading people astray with doctrines of demons. Scripture is about Jesus, as 2 Peter 3:17-18 states:

"Ye therefore, beloved, seeing ye know [these things] before, beware lest ye also, being led away with the error of the wicked, fall from your own stedfastness. But grow in grace, and [in] the knowledge of our Lord and Saviour Jesus Christ. To him [be] glory both now and for ever. Amen."

SCRIPTURE REFERENCED IN CONCLUSION

James 2:23 And the scripture was fulfilled which saith, Abraham believed God, and it was imputed unto him for righteousness: and he was called the Friend of God.

Romans 2:24 For the name of God is blasphemed among the Gentiles through you, as it is written.

Revelation 21:27 And there shall in no wise enter into it any thing that defileth, neither whatsoever worketh abomination, or maketh a lie: but they which are written in the Lamb's book of life.

SOURCES / REFERENCES

King James Version (KJV) of the Bible
All Scripture cited is from this source.

Michael D. Johnson MD. Human Biology Concepts and Current Issues. 5th Ed. Pearson Benjamin Cummings, San Francisco, CA. pp. 481-483.

David J. Stewart. Human Bodies and Celestial Bodies are Way Different. The Book Of Enoch EXPOSED! November 2006.http://jesus-is-savior.com/Wolves/book_of_enoch.htm.

Nephilim Nonsense on GracethruFaith.
Sunday, January 24th, 2016. Downloaded January 26th, 2016. https://gracethrufaith.com/ask-a-bible-teacher/how-could-angels-do-this/

Gigantism, Mosby's Medical Dictionary, 9th edition. © 2009, Elsevier
http://medical-dictionary.thefreedictionary.com/gigantism
[jigan'tizem] Etymology: L, gigas, giant. an abnormal condition characterized by excessive size and stature. It is caused most frequently by hypersecretion of growth hormone (GH) that occurs before the closure of the bone epiphyses; it occurs to a lesser degree in hypogonadism and in certain genetic disorders. Gigantism with normal body proportions and normal sexual development usually results from hypersecretion of GH in early childhood. Hypogonadism, by delaying puberty and closure of the epiphyses, may lead to gigantism. Excessive linear growth often occurs in males with more than one Y chromosome...

Nephilim Nonsense on RR Website
"Interesting E-mail Both the pro and the con Jan4"
[http://www.raptureready.com/index.phpDownloaded/
http://www.raptureready.com/rap37.html.

Nephilim Nonsense on Rapture Ready
Ron Graham. Strange Flesh Punishment – God Style.
Downloaded verbatim January 26th 2016.
http://www.raptureready.com/featured/graham/g147.html.

Graham. "The Gadarene Demoniac"
Downloaded verbatim Jan 26th, 2016.
http://www.raptureready.com/featured/graham/g54.html

Early Earth
Institute for Creation Research. http://www.icr.org/

Donald Wesley Patten. Catastrophism and the Old Testament The Mars-Earth Conflicts Pacific Meridian Pub Co; First Edition (September 1988)

Dr. Kent Hovind's website 2Peter3.com
https://2peter3.com/kent-hovind-canopy-theory-kjv-bible/

Genome Research
National Institute of Health (NIH) Human Genome Project (HGP) Research Institute
https://www.genome.gov/12011238

Institute for Creation Research. Numerous peer-reviewed scientific articles, several on Genome research.
http://www.icr.org

READER'S NOTES

Made in United States
Troutdale, OR
11/03/2024

24385028R00070